Praise for *Athena Dej*

Clifford Brooks' poetry's uniqueness blooms from its denial to conform to the befuddling or the politically correct. His poetry is raw, carved from an emotional and explosive force—by turns manic and somber, heartbroken and heart-strong. His work reflects a vast intellect, but he has nothing to prove, other than the fact that he is, in his moving through life, a ghost, anachronistic in his passion. Most of these poems are elegiac, outspoken, and even tortured. However, none are *tortuous*. There are no linguistic games here, other than deft metaphor and subtle aestheticizing—the ornaments a poet knows must adorn the work to distinguish itself from prose, poetry's brassy sister.

In this way, Brooks defies the conventions of many literary poets and creates a space for his own literariness, one borne from the romantic tradition of emotional recollection and powerful feeling, sometimes recollected in tranquility, sometimes confronted head-on with a bellicosity that can startle and surprise in interesting and often beautiful ways. Brooks is unafraid to bear the conflicts of his inner demons and angels—in doing so, he transcribes the freight he carries as a man both tethered to, and haunted by, his world of words.

—WILLIAM WRIGHT, author of *Tree Heresies*

In *Athena Departs: Gospel of a Man Apart,* Clifford Brooks tells us early on, "I reflect on the reasons / life refused to let me go." But his expansive poems are more than reflections, so much more. Brooks creates in his work places where the blues and philosophy both sing their songs of modern doubt and love, where downtown Athens, Georgia, can be home to Damon and Pythias but still have "Jackson's secondhand bookshop" with "collections written by Rilke, Neruda, and Simic," and where Granny and Dad and church and Grandfather and Momma share the world with Ovid and Odysseus, Penelope and Cupid and Old Man Scratch, Medusa and Thanatos and the Underworld.

—JON TRIBBLE, author of *And There is Many a Good Thing*

"We shall always be suspicious things to a species stuck in neutral," writes Clifford Brooks in his oracular collection, *Athena Departs: Gospel of a Man Apart*. Brooks' poems accelerate on the page with lyric beauty, allusions, raw honey sweetness, and country boy renaissance snap, through demonizing tunnels to expose nihilism, love, faith, and our broken down lives. But he reminds us of our strength along the way: "We flourish best in unforgiving weather." His poems hum with a haunting melody and impact with the emotional whirlwind of "a natural catastrophe." The centerline on Brooks' road may indeed be the "creator's urgency to be happy, or be nothing." These poems careen with wild inventiveness; steer us straight into "blades that slice away." Scream to this poet, *"Drive me."*

—TIM CONROY, author of *Theologies of Terrain*

There are storytellers, and there are stories. Occasionally, we find no distinction between them. This is the case with Clifford Brooks. In his new collection, *Athena Departs: Gospel of a Man Apart,* the narrative often becomes the narrator, and whatever lines we assign between teller and told become irrelevant. In this sense, these poems function the way mythology does—they offer us a way inward so that we can more easily navigate a way back out. The reverse is also true in that Brooks asserts our collective humanness while also praising our divine individuality.

Athena Departs: Gospel of a Man Apart is sexy in its ferocity and music, its insistence that we slow down and pay close attention to why we write our own myths, and how these will be carried close to the heart, or tossed dangerously into some storm. Brooks asks much of us in these new poems and he offers us his oaths, too. This is not a soft book, nor a safe one. Brooks does not once ask us to let go—rather, he invites us to settle in for long nights in the Southern stick and wet, where we might look up— and consider Olympus not so far after all.

—KELLI ALLEN, author of *Imagine Not Drowning*

3/17/18

Lauren,

Thank God you came with such love.
The love is forever.

[illegible signature]

Athena Departs: Gospel of a Man Apart

ATHENA DEPARTS

GOSPEL OF A MAN APART

Poems by Clifford Brooks

Kudzu Leaf Press

Marietta, Georgia

Kudzu Leaf Press
P.O. Box 2076
Marietta, GA 30061
kudzuleafpress.com

kudzuleafpress@gmail.com

Some of the poems in this collection also appear in *Exiles of
Eden* by Clifford Brooks, a limited-edition chapbook published
by Kudzu Leaf Press in 2017.

ISBN: 978-0-9995304-1-2

Library of Congress Control Number: 2017958651

Author photo by James Polfuss

Cover design by Jackie A. Gentile

Font: Georgia

for Momma, Andy Whitehorne,
Keith Hughes, James Johnson, Mike Strickland,
Tracy Kincaid, Russell Howard, D. L. Yancey, II
and the Southern Collective Experience

with thanks to William Wright

Contents

Foreword

Clifford Brooks carries the fire. There's a passion in his work, and from what I've seen of him over the years, you'll find the same in his life, his every day a pool of gasoline waiting for the match, and it's hard not to feel that flame catch on and spread into my own life whenever I read his poetry or speak or write to him. His intensity for the work that goes into writing and promoting the work of others, and his dogged determination for poetic perfection even while knowing perfection is unobtainable, inspires us who know his work well.

With *Athena Departs: Gospel of a Man Apart*, we have another collection born of that endless struggle, in which Brooks puts into words what life has put into him—the roadblocks and majesties, the miracles and knock-out punches, all elevated to a plane where his poems croon with a decadent cadence that's playful yet rich with purpose, as in his poem "After Rock-n-Rolla Lover Talk":

> *The elastic nature of words, their wickedness and flair,*
> *slipped into Athens last night*
> *to help cajole a wildly good girl.*
>
> The ridges of us fall soft
> against long talks
> that speak of us
> sharing a bed and blueberry pancakes.
>
> Snug, the navel is your epicenter
> where there's Vishnu and a small forest cabin.

His wordplay dances on the page and imbues the reality of love and loathing with an arcane recklessness, an obsession realized without any shame. Poem after poem Brooks champions this kind of fierce devotion, this kind of life, and as one progresses through the collection one realizes Brooks is building a mythology.

Poets worth their salt are able to create a world, a geography, a history, a magic that all form a unique mythology, recognizable as a fingerprint. Brooks has accomplished this over the course of his body of work. Yet, by "mythology" I certainly don't mean "lies" or "legends" or "prettied up half-truths" that sound falsely or absurdly heroic or tragic. While otherworldly beings dapple a few of these poems, readers will find concepts such as an eldest son's lack of conscience and his momma's undying hope.

In his first book, *The Draw of Broken Eyes & Whirling Metaphysics,* Brooks is a frightened child who wept over a broken heart all his fault. Here, in *Athena Departs: Gospel of a Man Apart,* there is a man firm in himself. Brooks' mind is a maze made of dirt roads and skyscrapers. His balance of grit and glory, of regret and defiance, his ability to let both coexist in the same poem is enviable, as found in "Promise to Momma":

There's a debt to deal with
from damage done
to my wrists.

Yet the scars ensure
I don't misplace the memory
of your undeserved sorrow.
You won't weep in the rain again,
Momma,

and my veins will be clean tomorrow.
Saint of a self-destructive son,
you instinctively let my Hyde slide,
but I shall not.
I cannot.

The line dividing aching realities and ephemeral fables are blurred in this mythology, blended with his accessible style, erudition, and an Old Testament temperament, creating a modern Southern gothic in which truth is a buried treasure and suffering is the map we follow to find it.

I say we follow Brooks as he sings old spirituals around Devil's Pond. In that town there is a blues bar where angels rest their wings and whisper confessions to the last Southern son. Between sets, Old Man Scratch uses a slide guitar to squeeze forgiveness out of six strings in hopes heaven will have him home. The poet's heart is no longer off-beat, and love is the light that leads him to the sliding glass door of Elysium.

James H. Duncan, author of *What Lies in Wait*

.

I shall seize Fate by the throat; it shall certainly not bend and crush me completely.

—LUDWIG VAN BEETHOVEN

If your daily life seems poor, do not blame it; blame yourself that you are not poet enough to call forth its riches; for the Creator, there is no poverty.

—RANIER MARIE RILKE, *Letters to a Young Poet*

Still here I carry my old delicious burdens,
I carry them, men and women, I carry them with me
    wherever I go,
I swear it is impossible for me to get rid of them,
I am fill'd with them, and I will fill them in return.

—WALT WHITMAN, "Song of the Open Road"

In the Beginning

there were two callused hearts.

[Early dawn brought distraction, labor,
and a lack of luster
pharmaceutical companies adore.
Last night saw black dogs,
heard the gasps of a panicked child,
struck dumb the boisterous voice.]

. . .

At noon you said:
Get over here and drive me!

I spent hours with you
lost, boozy, knowing you were thinking
of someone else.
We sped in a thoroughbred
until tears were chased behind
the moon.

Gordon, calmest of man's best friends,
took us to the river
by a path of pink hyacinth
hidden behind a low stone wall.
We sat near a spot where turtles sun.
You: *Do you need your little notebook?*
[No. No, I don't.]

The supper we shared
was served by a Lebanese man
sporting bad teeth and good Mexican food.
Our new evening got topped off
with tequila and kisses.

You said:
I like you too much. I don't need to feel
this affectionate blood.
Remember that there are others.

That's fine, dark-haired, frightened one.
My days are a malady
where I am thrown asunder in time.
I do not know the day.
I am not aware of tomorrow's appointments.

In the face of all evenings
kin to our memory,
I am cognizant of only this encounter,
this football game,
the breath before I leave.

Remember how I said before,
as I do now:
I have grown beyond wanting
anything
from you.

The Abandonment of Another Alice

The morning runs over me
like a petulant child.

In the hum
between guitar strings,
I see your face
all Irish,
on fire.

Through my hankering
for something new,
I am hung up
on how to skip out
on you.
As an anaconda to any
sweet, living thing,
it's a predictable
torture.

Due to the vexing
vertebrae in my lower half,
today is a jerky dance.
I've stopped paying attention
to the absence
of a conscience.
There are a dozen
unheard messages
from you
I won't open.
I've said hateful things.

This will remain unfinished business.
The man you've seen
is a jabberwocky

without willful ill.
I shall still
abandon you, Alice.

Bella's Ballad

You said: *Business has made you cruel. I can't be the woman you need.*

For the last seven months, civility has not been my best suit. In the beginning, I watched you sleep while making sure your son had blankets, and your daughter was safe. I missed you while still in the same house. I forgot I lived without children. I was on time for things. We were mitosis made to maintain our passionate design; happiness, with its delicate symmetry, snuck in. That night in my room will remind me science was on our side, too.

I called you Bella. You, a classic shape that urged me to cast you as a virgin from Venice. I witnessed you in your deepest thought, and when I asked what you wondered, you'd whisper, *Nothing.* Later on, you told me, *We are a team; you're not alone anymore.* That doesn't seem to be. You—the home, here, family—a family that now finds itself without me.

In the waking nights I know as normal, you found our cause for breakage—unsettling as the crackling sound of kindling. We almost settled, and then the seasons changed. *In January, all of this: the success, the devotion to provide—it was for you. Now, all of this: the continuation, the means to stability—it is a financially-sound distraction.*

Machiavelli's mindset is my mainstay. It is not what I want for you. You are the bright lilacs left in a house God built for girls with good intentions. My room is brash, unkempt. The thresholds I cross shouldn't damn you, too. Like prophets and lovers, in us was an intimacy both gospel and gluttonous. The cosmos doesn't condemn you, nor do I.

I was too erratic to sleep consistently, too frenzied to think about food *consistently*, and vented my vanity without thinking you would rather be true to our comfort, hold hands, and say it all, every syllable, in silence. I was not aware of the incident that invited my eviction. I never said that the hills can't have high IQs. Still, you have nothing to lose. Before we limped into the field where nothing can grow, I worried I would plant something despicable in you. *It is a good thing I didn't, darlin'.*

When we last looked at each other, I had a hunch the house we pretended was ours was no longer mine. *Pisces, we funny, conflicted fish feel the facts before angels can tip us off.* Intuitive, my eyes immediately etched the images of your front porch, beneath it where dogs stay dry; the uneven pavement; your ponytail stressfully off center: all of it remembered as you made haste to be rid of me.

The Taurus bull of you follows the familiar. Instead of growing dull, I decide to become an eloquent beast, purge the plans that sang so sweetly, and call about another apartment, empty, in another city. Mourning songs go on too long. This story closes with the blessed hum of brevity. Only we will hear our hymn on wind special to March. It is a gust that guarantees I will not forget: *I should have been smarter.*

A Father Sits with His Son

Every Sunday morning,
Dad brings his old dog
to the big house.
The hound bounds
toward the tool shed
while Pop and I lean
against white pillars.
A few old folks across the street
shuffle single file
into church.

We do not mock the flock
or their minister.
An ancient man glances
with disdain our way.
I don't give a shit.
There is nothing new
regarding redemption.
I will not be judged.

We celebrate the Holy Spirit
with a smoke.
I quote Don Quixote,
and Dad whispers,
Amen.
We share no guilt,
nor position to defend.

Dad and I are glad
to get this chance
to sit, speak,
recline behind pecan trees.
We listen to wind
without want

for the least whisper.
All that matters:
The solitude shall not kill me.

Two hundred acres of azalea
crown the landscape I keep
while dad drinks beer.
The whole of it is split by a river
that washes our feet.
There is no forgiveness
from the family.
Their names are not important.

In vicious loops,
I relive the past.
Dad's acceptance of me
will not last.
In this moment
my old man says to me:
"We've had our good days,
son,
and we've had our bad."

Blues 'Round Midnight

Robert Johnson jacked up
my love
of brown liquor.
The affection affixes me
to the sprawling agony of the Furies.
But there ain't no blues
Beelzebub can bounce
off me
that the right woman
can't wave away.

Numb: Night terrors have me
harangued and haunted.
Gums receding, mentally rickety;
the recollection of losing a girlfriend
to Christ doesn't develop
into a malady of doubt.
He can have her.
She's married with five kids now.
I never adopt another's anxiety.
When guilt gets in my guts,
I gotta get goin'.

Little old ladies are precious
in pews, praying for me.
The music never changes.
It's a tender language.
They are a prayer list.
Such a small, quiet room
where people think of the dead
and sniffle.

Held down hard
by heavy breaths,
I insist my grief

is the stabbing sprawl
of what pain is
the day after vodka
sucked from a plastic bottle.

Amore and addiction (their taste
is exactly the same):
I sew them up in a burlap sack,
then sink it into the Oconee.

I reflect on all the reasons
life refused to let me go.
There were
three winters where
my resolve failed like Hector.
An antidote was absent.
I was absent.

In the ache of being no one,
my ego left a contusion
still etched on my face.
I have forgone
trying to find its cause.
It remains elusive.

Still, I'll still stay up,
awake but unaware
beyond the burden
my mind can bear.
Every day I decide
to ignore my rusty pipes,
and deem the migraines
divine.

In time there will be quiet,
and my qualms with worry
will be seeds of escape.
I cannot wait
for a clean slate
sung to Etta James'
"Don't Explain."

Saturday Chaconne

Damon and Pythias
shake off Syracuse,
and brush their shoulders clean.
In downtown Athens
short skirts scoot us up one street,
then left on College Avenue.
Brothers head into a hookah bar.

Jackson's secondhand bookshop
contains collections
by Rilke, Neruda, and Simic
whose woo factor
hit their limit.
Now they're here
with scribbled epitaphs
that whisper: *The heart doesn't
always win.*

Nor is family loyal to their tortured son.
So, I decide to inscribe my insanity
in a tattoo venue.
Now, the motto of my family's melancholy
is carved into muscle over time.
The blood spilt in that chair
is theirs as much as mine.
Finem Respice
is forever
on my left arm.

On Four Fat Tires, we careen
into the old decor of New Orleans.
This eatery has been renamed,
but it's still the same.
Dad sits inside, smiling:
My old man
is always smiling.

We watch the waning sun
set across Broad Street
over the Arches
that urge us to understand
that the ache of youth passes,
age has a slanted perspective,
and nothing is wasted with good company.

As evening winks in,
a dogwood lets petals drift.

After Rock-and-Rolla Lover Talk

The elastic nature of words, their wickedness and flair,
slipped into Athens last night
to help cajole a wildly good girl.

The ridges of us fall soft
against long talks
that speak of us
sharing a bed and blueberry pancakes.

Snug, the navel is your epicenter
where there's Vishnu and a small forest cabin.
In this incendiary evening,
we are not self-conscious.

There is only calm where organs lay wet.

Hypothetical Date with Calypso

There is no better night
than one when Cupid refuses his fickle flight.
I do not want intimacy.
There is no room for brooding
or dreams.
Yet, due to the DNA of fate,
we attend the same soiree.

I smoke.
The smell irritates you,
but you refuse
to be difficult.
(I light another in delight.)
You make it my last,
by lifting both my hands
to dance.

You stay to say you might
want to talk
in spite
of the fear you feel.
Tonight we are owls,
or blue herons—delicate fowl.
Our eyes agree to feast
too fast.

Brilliant, you. Resilient, you:
I glance at your breasts
when it appears
you are not paying attention:
That's a trick.
No man before forty
is cool enough to catch cleavage
without claws coming out.
However,
I never claimed to be clever.

Breathe, my sweet,
breathe because
deep, deep, deep
beneath the ocean of us
there is a reef that keeps
the outcome of our courtship
a secret.

My fixation on your flesh
forces me to fidget
like a hound-hunted fox.
You kiss my cheek,
and compliment my socks.
Woman, you don't want this.
Even if I told you
how alone
loving me leaves a lady,
you'd stay.

My heart is not a cruel knot,
but what beats is not made of muscle.
God clamped a clock inside
that no one bothered to wind.

The Seeds of Our (Un)Becoming

Meticulously fashioned
from fuchsias and sadism,
our anatomy is anything
but innocent.
Our oval soul is cold
because compassion is a corpse,
and its canines chew
me from restful roots.
In insidious soil, this man
stands:
the Patron Saint of Chance.

You see, and need to believe,
we are only dualities
of a coin purloined but no one needs.
You are the hangman's tree,
and I am the sun eclipsed
by a stupid moon.

Stop stalling and help
me decide
the best way to let this die.

A few days ago, we were precious stones
flown on broad wings,
preoccupying the hallowed skies
of happiness.
Now, I want to be rid, and free,
of you.

Your scheme leaves a suspicion
in my mind like a lesion,
compassion's cancer.
You are the only question
with no answer.

So I say,
Go.
You should fly
with another,
younger flock.

Two Old Men

Two old men
fix my washing machine.
They tell me this model falls short
of the more reliable brands.
The bill makes my head hurt.

I half-expect
some Great Depression
philosophy
for such a nasty sum.

No luck.

The condescending fucks
take my cash
and rumble off
in a battered Chevrolet.

The Lady is a Lark

As you test the bathroom's
acoustics,
I pretend to sleep
so as not to wreck this rarity.

You are singing.

Your voice
flutters vibrato:

Due to you
my chaos is lost
like rain on the wings
of a wren.

I know you don't believe me.
Why be frail?
It's lunacy
to think you will fail.

Please,
Sing!

Memoir of a Madman

Beneath acne scars,
barely dodging prison bars,
and the spell of a slide guitar,
there is the molten marrow
of a man.

You: Come here,
and peer into the mirror
without fear,
and I'll prove you're
a fool.

Disaster does not ease into a quiet evening
to help meek men
maintain weak excuses.
Nostalgia is a narcotic
not worth a nickel.

If you're on the market
for a makeshift miracle,
never sit for a meal
with a holy man . . .
unless he has a dark history.
Confessions are always
gibberish to saints.
Devils do the real time.
Reconcile your yearning
for Yahweh with a long yawn.

Your spirit will be moved
only by heat stroke
at summer revival.
Speaking in tongues is as close

to celebrity
as those circus tent
idiots will ever get.
I thought such bad behavior
was drunk, not divine.

Horror is an honor
when administered
on another.

I am a Buddhist-bar fight
of beliefs.
I like the stoic cause of Christ,
while still stay close to cults of reason.
There is little time to sleep.
I thumb my barbed,
wooden prayer beads
and wait.

The bane of bad faith
is a sack of snakes held out
to any congregation.
I trade the dunce's fedora
with any wretch
who recognizes that rattle
as the song of a savior
instead of insanity.

As a monk,
I cautiously
carve cathedrals
with sharp tools kept strong
by street-scraped knuckles.
I stop for every long
hearse ride home,

because the earth groans
with each corpse
returned too soon.

The Honest Oath of Our Shower

This shower is always warm,
so wash off who came before.
My water is yours.
In here you'll never stand
behind me,
that cold tile at your back.

I think, like love,
wanting is eternal.
Seldom found in one,
both
are born in you.

I adore your honest hips,
your bad habits,
the midnight romps
that get the neighbors
riled up.
But you're cute and convincing enough
to keep the cops
from coming inside.

July 4th Parade

On atomic-hot asphalt
parade floats
are an American obsession.
Sweat bunches Dad's underwear.
Yellow chewing gum is stuck to his shoe.
One of the children
has broken loose.

Mom is barely there.
She ignores family to sneer.
Perky cheerleaders are murder.
Back then she was a siren,
in the days previous to the PTA.

Football players and police
throw cheap candy
kids fight over.
The band is out of key.
Dad wants to go home.
Mother, slack-shouldered,
is bitter.

In the Hunger of Long Hours

I entertained 20-somethings,
and several single moms,
without the want
to suffer despite them.
I don't lead
on bended knee,
nor wait for a queen
to set me free.

Instead, an emptiness
stretches the chasm
of your exit.
I'm parched on hateful sand;
silently sworn the hollow man.

Pretty, silly girl,
I pretended
each princess
enhanced my joyless sky,
but the immediate relief
of their absence
insisted
they didn't.

Please restrain
your resentment,
pity,
and/or envy.
Those betties
acted as a sanctuary.
Each one staved off
the sickness
of soullessness.

I act the hero,
but have helpless hands.
I have no soul.
Instead I let a mammoth
resolve take root.

In the crush
of scar tissue you
hit, bit, and beat
into my spine and waistline,
there is a gnawing need
to retrieve *everything*.

As My Mind Wanders, Seasons Change

Under a rouge moon,
the day's last silver
is snuffed out.
An old sky expires.
My breath is fog
in the porch light.
Ahead is an expanse
that embraces
a better, solitary existence.

Geese are in noisy motion,
a fuss before winter.
On this year's last leg,
a sanguine evening's end
is sealed in by the wind.
However, it's not the clime
that causes my decline.
I shiver due to the
shrew who sits
on the sofa,
inside.

A Noble Death

I want what Ovid achieved,
or Odysseus' watery end.
Oh, to have my own Ithaca!
When this man's thread is cut,
I'll go without
the over-worked nurse.

If not a writer or warrior,
allow me to leave
as the laughing grandfather.
One well-read gent
with a quick joke,
and candy in his pocket.
Let me check out cutting wood.

I refuse a sterile room
that smells of bleach and senility.
Death gets bored, waiting
as tubes sustain me.
I'll ghost myself
before that
addled disassembly.

A Legion of Wolves Within Me

An intelligent hell would be better than a stupid paradise.
　　　　　　　—VICTOR HUGO, *Ninety-Three*

Laced in lavender rhododendron,
the lake of this estate
is fed from springs
that thread beneath
an impromptu parking lot.
My fingers linger
over the back legs of a grasshopper
while my business partner
puts speakers in place.

Today,
we are music men
rented to render this wedding
a waltz instead of a wreck.
I don't walk far with my guitar
until a trail, bent like the tail
of a water dragon,
opens to a meadow.
In its center is a shoddy stage
accented with iron deer.

This hootenanny
is plenty better than abandonment.
My bitter sentiment is buried
in the deep of Sharpe Top's shadow.
No one senses my sorrow.
The bride and groom
are barely grown.
I wish all their skies stay blue
as they say, *I do.*

Our band plays
for the many who stay.
Not too far away
brothers, or aunts, or cousins
stroll in lazy swirls,
circling the food
like starving crows,
or pigeons, or sparrows.

Hours pass, good people dance,
and then night begs us to be gone.
I ease an escape, but find
a murder of unwed women
unwilling to let me,
ladies in waiting
unaware this man
is unmade.

No. Let me go.
I want the wind
to blow me home solo,
without guilt or girls in tow.

A Day in Marble Hill

The weather is sickly,
and a neglected koi pond
needs the leaves raked out.
My sloth has no excuse.
This malaise quells the urge
to cut grass,
repaint the shutters,
or get a divorce.

Someone decides
to shoot a shotgun
as if today is the only day to do it.
The neighbor's dog
is half-wild.
Our only road
to the main drag
is wicked,
and isn't kept up by the county.

A busted-up truck
roars east,
and west,
then east again.

Outside this lopsided house,
there's a weakly-rigged swing set
where you tried to explain
why you never wear
the only wedding ring
I could afford.

Scotch, Scuffles, and Sermons

This Sunday in North Georgia,
I pump gas,
and wonder if my momma
knows I'm dodging an hour of dogma.
The Deity and I are free
to sleep without a fiery end.

A welcome distraction: two ratty kids
wrestle over a chocolate bar.
The shouting grows profane.
The father is an arm's length away.

Gas stations make bank now
selling newly-sanctioned Sunday booze.
I imagine rooms of worship
where they worry and wish
their flocks away from desperation.
I do not judge.
I'm pew-absent as much as those children.

Youth being
most like beasts,
the boys begin
beating each other like men.
They bleed into broken pavement.
I acknowledge these events,
absolved.

Meeting Old Man Scratch (1)

[I knew it was a bad day
first thing this morning.

Old Man Scratch stood on my stoop,
all snarly like an angry father
irate about me coming home
three weeks late.
That burly goat's got nothing
but time,
while we both know
my dirt-road rambling
is ticking low,
and well into the red.]

. . .

Let me speak it now, fellow Exiles of Eden:
Time barely gets us by.
When Scratch calls in
his due,
our meek majority
weeps, screams,
and scampers.
Kind folks,
he knows where the soul
goes,
and all the mortal alleys
in which your mind can hide.
Be still,
listen.

The bard's most brutal trick:
An orgasmic trumpet-blown breath,
booming—swooning the room,

briefly touching your spirit—
blinding the crowd so the vagrant-poet
can vanish
as if his clothes were sewn
from soot.
Trust me, it's for the best.
Consequences of his coming
are inevitably messy.
Maybe the bluesman left a baby,
or something else not quite on the level.
If so, it's damning,
but certainly not *evil*.

Bringing it back:
Under Spanish moss, smoking,
the Tyrant of Temptation
is aware we see the same,
inglorious end.
There has been laughter, nicotine rings,
and a few unmentionable flings
between us.
He and I go back,
but not like Faust
or rowdy Hank Williams, Sr.
This kinship is linked to a promise,
close to my skin,
rarely friendly.

Looking out over the unpainted railing,
I stand with feet
unshaken by the presence of iniquity.
It won't be easy to waltz me
off this rock,
but my bony body
will buckle
before I can noodle another swindle.

So I grin, tap dance
around the sorrow of what's on the way,
man up.

Just then:
Scratch takes out a silver pocket watch,
and pretends to wave away
the blaze
he brought with him.
Suddenly solemn, he turns his yellow irises on me:
You're burnin' through virtue
faster than the good you do, boy.

I remember; I can still clearly see:
We hung out when the world,
more than once before,
waltzed near annihilation,
but we're not laughing now.
Scratch gently pats my shoulder,
then bends into a mocking bow.
Finally, in a sizzle, the sinister son
slips out of sight.

Like all early morning bad news,
Old Scratch's time with me today
will make for a hard night.

Meeting Old Man Scratch (2)

Old Man Scratch
seems sat-back-easy
on my front porch,
slouched in a chair
where my grandmother snapped
green beans
during times
men were more crossroads wise.

Predestination or not,
Granny
knew her eldest grandson
is one
who would welcome calamity
for more celebrity
than he can carry.
There's black magic around
my enchanted
choice of occupation,
but it is the music
that keeps a fire in men.

Still sitting—smiling,
the Saint of Pimps
appears almost blameless.
Iniquity reclines in a reverie
that seems complete and content,
like the first time
I kissed a girl.

. . .

Our shadows look lean,
and stretch out
like the front legs
of a brown recluse.
In the sun, they seem the same.
Barely a breathable distance
between us at any time,
it's deliciously brutal.

It is nothing new:
There's too much truth in
Georgia-poet voodoo
to let me forget
my momma
and a monster
have an equal share
of my tombstone stock.

There's a tally taken
for every untouched flower
I pick, promise forever,
then only keep a single evening.
There are spells in ink
up both arms
to squirm a few more weeks
of Sundays;
to stay in the sun
until my wendigo wises up.

Mad-rushing memories
have immortalized motels in Athens
and romances in Rome.
This restlessness
is from knowing

there's a hard time
to get on with.

I try not to make my folks
fuss too much.
I've got one's good sense,
and the other's talent
for thinking around it.
Morality is best left to Milton.
I've got a one-hundred dollar bill
and golden fiddle built-in
when the world, during a rave,
or Easter morning, ends
on a high note.

. . .

Digging back into the Devil,
my only two cents sneers:
Bring on the Rapture!
I'm sure Paradise is boring
if all the women there are pure.
I've got better things to do
than worry about fear, forgiveness,
and you.

The Sweetness of a Long Bath

Our imbalance
is a byproduct
of my bent cerebellum
left too long
to itself.

So, I stayed awake all day
and had our inhibitions darned
like an old sweater.
The good sheets and I
(and you)
are
now spotless.

Maybe you'll
cook Thai tonight.
Later we'll rest well,
ready to take
any new strife
in stride
tomorrow.

This evening,
I will clean the countertops,
then draw your bath,
and these hands will heal your
sore muscles.
When the lights wink out,
we can pray for whatever you want.

The world
stays starched and fresh
because of our
equal faith in spirit and flesh.

The Last Wispy Gypsy

There is a shelter off Sunshine Road where the wind brought from Tennessee tickles the neck, and slips between me and my t-shirt. The Wispy Gypsy sits beside me and guides my ill-prepared id into the palace of her smallest mouth.

Outside the gypsy's bedroom window, one weeping willow is mashed-in with an arrangement of herbs to be harvested for white magic. A Japanese maple looks out of place among its plain, leafy cousins, like Gandhi selling fake Super Bowl tickets in Times Square. The land is her curve, her swerve, and the nexus of her intelligent conversation. *It's the final virtuous thought I'll have this evening.*

Virtue: That is nonsense, boring morality, a negative flesh worn in the city. It is scoffed and skinned off before I cross the threshold of A Delicate Balance. There is no worry once the door swings closed, shoes off, and pajamas put on. There are no cats, and only one hound comes around when a harvest moon is highest in the unfeeling sky. *Motorcycles are no strangers to my vehicle, blue in the day, silver in the shade, whose owners show up in various states of sober—as I am apt to do.*

A lava lamp goes all night as the Wispy Gypsy furiously fights the forest back from taking over her front yard. Nearly always nude, she rattles the rafters with an unapologetic, bawdy voice. That sound and its maker, the long moan and the minx, are out to worship Gaia's unfading freedom worn by women. I stagger into her to heal, to quell the squall from notoriety for better jokes, curlier hair, and firmer resolve. Her homemade remedies, spicy from serrano, open my stomach. Two spoons of honey then finally fit between fevered lips. She woos this wolf getting grey in his beard; her thighs insist me into her den, to the bedroom, bumping us into a bed big enough for two, and my ego. *When in doubt, don't assume it's best to go slow.*

Rubbing noses, we coax out more nighttime, linger, star-bathe with our pupils wide open, glazed against the dawn. One-night-into-the next-day-into-the-next night, she's brutally honest, deeply-rooted in the hillside, too trusting but tough. I am gangly, and guilty of wanderlust. No one keeps watch down the dirt road leading back to pavement. Kind criminals often come up to take back our news. Our weekend-long watusi is witnessed by errant crows that finally, fully, cry: *Thank you!* This is a *Hell Yeah Hallelujah* that reminds us temptation is not always tainted by torture in some second life. *That is lazy introspection. It is the seed of starvation.*

Sparrows sit in threes, distant, curious as to what is so wonderful about love: *Love, love, love?* The earth cradling us is soft and clean as my thoughts once were. When I inevitably drive away, I douse the ground with Indian nickels in homage to the tempest that may talk in sailor's slang, but remains sweet to every stranger. It is religious, necessary, a Texas Two Step with an allegory in a short skirt. *As with every allegory, there is an end, then the lesson learned that leaves at least one card in the deck feeling misplaced.*

A Dream of Pawpaw

Pawpaw was a proud farmer.
A warrior in Africa,
at home he was
wrought from the earth in overalls.
Burly-strong and big as his land,
I am part of his legacy.

After the Second Great War,
he came home
but couldn't hunt.
There was too much blood
gouged out in Europe.

Set him down.
Let us meet like strangers.
The photos are faded.
I have been to his grave.

Rest me beside his bones,
he, the unknown kin.
Rush those strong arms
around me.
Pillow my cowardice atop his chest.

Thanatos:
Let loose my Pawpaw!
Bear me a moment with him.
Mark the man a hero,
then release his soul to me.

I Finally Slept Last Night

I sleep to slip into a space
not scarred by need or family
or the strife of bad business
done well.

Robbed by a long winter,
my distaste for discontent
runs deep.
Yet, yesterday's gray
is pushed away
to make room
for a man too busy
for burden.

Young women clamor
like otters
over each other.
Fathers make noise
like teenagers.
Laughter lingers in
and spins off
like leaf-splintered sun.

No more, I said among family.
No more!
Brooding is given a break.
Surly harpies hang back.
They recognize
the futility
of their attack.
In the meantime,
my eyes on tonight,
I will sleep
like worry never was.

Letter to the Editor

Hear my problem,
Old Man:
I wear the world,
anguished by its lacking.

I write.
I write so others
might wail as well.

They don't.
I do.

That's the problem.

The Keeper of Grief

(for Sosha Pease)

Case files are photocopied
on wax paper
with ink drawn
from
formaldehyde.
My job is to log
a child's long haul,
and scribble down
the basics,
after they've
been mauled.
It is an act
of incessant hindsight.

I am an intruder,
the poorest man's confessor.
Childhood curls, hopeful girls:
You sleep in shit so thick
it's slick on my shoes.
Daddy's lullabies are
prison terms,
cigarette burns,
and unwanted daughters.
The un-orphaned
orphans
have faces
vacant
in the important
places.

Tonight,
my black robe is faded
on its hook,

white collar frayed.
I pray.
New dawn is new hate.
I point out the liar,
the arsonist,
the thief.
I am the hypocrite,
the idiot,
the Keeper of Grief.

Promise to Momma

You told me Tuesday it was time
to simmer for my heavy mind's sake.
A son shouldn't be so good
at makin' his momma's heart break.
I won't say how I got lost
just yet,
because hell is listenin'
for me to spill my secret.

Don't go blamin' bad luck,
because a restless soul is my undoin'.
I'm overdrawn at the Bank of Legion
due to the price of a few sinister seasons,
so I sing spirituals
and think of sermons I've missed.
There's a debt to deal with
from damage done
to my wrists.

Yet the scars ensure
I don't misplace the memory
of your undeserved sorrow.
You won't weep in the rain again,
Momma,
and my veins will be clean tomorrow.
Saint of a self-destructive son,
you instinctively let my Hyde slide,
but I shall not.
I cannot.

When I sit down with my misdeeds,
it's obvious all I'm gonna do
is fall short of a picket fence,
the wife of a quiet life,
and you.

Samson Regained

Once Samson was shaved
and betrayed by beauty.
Regardless, he refused to renounce
his faith as foolish.
Before he could see it coming,
our love-dumb warrior couldn't weave,
bob, or duck
Delilah's deception.
It is the martyr's luck.
Indecent delight
gouged out his eyes,
and memories of blue skies.

Lord knows it is understandable.
The man was all muscle
with little meat beneath
his mullet.

Nevertheless, it is not about academics—
Samson's innocence is no excuse
for her cruelty.
The fault is the fiend found
in the heart of a fraudulent Medea.
Unlucky love is life!
Samson's sweet disposition
died, dour, hacked out
and scattered
into a sea thought
the property of Poseidon.

However, the predicament
insisted there was no time
for superstition.
(It takes a weightless soul

to exile a skank
who sliced it up.)
Samson would survive the plight
placed on a savior.
Samson sees simply his
single regret suffer instead.

Now: *Listen,*
in my reshaping of this story,
Samson didn't stay securely chained.
There's no prize for the dead-end
of being pummeled
beneath pillars.
My biblical brute becomes
a thriving lion-fighter,
and swings his arms
like angry archangels.

In the space left by self-sacrifice,
Samson decides
to stick around, set up shop,
and invites his city
to witness Led Zeppelin,
lazy days on white beaches,
and democracy.
The Deity of Getting
the Hard Shit Done
restores Samson's sight.

. . .

Remember discarded Delilah?
She is undead, in a distant slum,
doomed to wear

a halter-top hewn from Samson's old hair.
Vanity has affixed her in infamy
as a vicious warning
the world whispers,
in hisses,
as if *speaking* of her
invokes a virus.

The Lasting Melody Made of God

(for Fahim Ali)

When our species decided
to discover
an accessible deity,
one song was slung across
an abyss
we suspected
was only dead space.

What we uncovered
was another culture.
Together, we articulated
earth's universal tongue,
still humming in uncommon notation.
Now it is our bloodless kinship.

There's more
beyond our mindscape
than oblivion
or bondage.

Genesis split
the original, gentle night
with a mother-of-mornings.
Our instincts
naturally listened
for chords
that quelled chaos,
not caused it.

The facts are not far-fetched:
Prayers progressed into psalms.
We grew from a fertile,
gospel womb.
Standing upright,

we resonated as the rhapsody
of God's first words:
We are all kept safe
in the Old Man's hands.
Our darkest deeds
are blown free,
like dandelion seeds in a gale.

In the event
my concept of soul
lacks enough evidence
to earn your certainty,
rely on reason.
The only theology
worth knowing is:
None of this
is meaningless.

An Ode to Southern Sons, and Uncivil Rest

To wisdom, beauty, and truth:
We are souls strapped down
by the malicious hands of man.
Do not judge our dreams
for making selfish realities.
We flourish best in unforgiving weather.

This Sisyphus has a story,
sans a stone to roll.
Pull up a stool,
sit still,
and abandon your albatross.
Buy a beer distilled
in guilt and gritty with ocean silt.
Good? Let's get it on.
The fact I feel firm to follow is:
Our innermost selves
are smashed every day
against our addiction to suffer.

Hobgoblins hunt us down
and steal our resolve.
All of us are blunted by the hour.

We want, *we yearn*
for the best yesterday that yawns empty.
We remember and wish wrong:
To have a reason to disregard
our inevitable, unremarkable
retreat into the earth.

Of course,
we discover our bravest face

out on the ocean.
So, go!
Pull up anchor and set sail.
Seek out a storm
and see what's
in your gut.

Making nice with the facts
is always a maelstrom.
Honesty is most like Christ.
As a sacrament, scripture
is tattooed
down my arms,
and abandonment
across my chest,
and Brutus burned into my back.
I am a battlefield.

Sex and Sweet Tea

The last three hours
have been a bawdy vacation.
In the heat of each other,
we howled in our favorite positions.
Now, we've come to a salty elation.

Our dirty dialogue fed
your need to devour me,
and my sly fingers
made you compliant.

Age, time, settling:
We are none of these,
nor do they dictate to us
when to temper
our assaults
on the boudoir.

After riot-inspired sex
and a few tugs of tobacco,
I follow you
down the hall
for a peach-flavored dessert
and sweet tea.

Between us
and our kitchen window,
the air is wound up
in sandalwood incense.
Outside,
a lazy summer sun

slinks towards the bottom
of a soft,
red Southern sky.

Murderer Returned

The courtroom cradles
a crowd held in place
by macabre fascination.
Old women hiss about bad blood.
A preacher skulks in the back.
Many seem to hold their breath,
anticipating agony.

Apparently,
this gossiping sewing circle
gathers this afternoon
to share the room
with a beast.
The bailiff points to
a family that files in
with hopes to find their fiend
still rotting.

The maniac's son
is a policeman.
He's away from the others,
silent,
slump-shouldered,
thick hands clenched.

Zipped up in
inmate orange,
the murderer,
an old, chaperoned baboon
chink,
chink,
chinks
to center stage.

Grunting,
smelling the sad-sick air,
the prisoner peers out,
and sees me spy his condition:
He is an uncomplicated, ruddy skull.
I stare at the product
of an addicted end,
feel nothing.

Lawyers nod, whisper,
the judge is satisfied,
then the bones led away.
A reporter skips out.
Friends, unnerved,
chuckle nervously.

The policeman remains in his seat.
He's a boy disinherited, again.
The heavy son
is slump-shouldered,
thick hands
no longer clenched.
I bet it is because
the boy
let his daddy go.

The Summer of C

I.

Long, Quiet Weeks:

When the corners of your office
take over lazy days, your all-time,
your patience
to put up with one more word,
I will quarrel with being quiet.

II.

The Only Weekend Away:

Bees drink from a pool
left by a stream
that wore its way
through great rocks
to be here.
The sun is tempered
by today's soft storm.

Behind you,
there is a place
where a space in the forest
pours out a tongue of water.
The murmur of it
is the only sound
aside from cicadas.

We play with your pooch,
look for tadpoles,
and decide

to plant snapdragons at home.
You tiptoe
from one safe stone
to another.

III.

Final Score:

Ours was a fiercely flawed,
final score.
That terrific implosion
snuffed out anything endearing.
Yet, early on, you admitted
I might not
want to expect miracles.
For me to argue
with you
is like barking at the moon.

The tempest in me
is a temporary thing.
I suffer a soul's frenzy
that's frustrated by what you
consider fun.
My smell is honeysuckle-sweet
because I'm
more molten this summer
than last.
I am sorry
you were swallowed
in my abyss.

There are a few
evening hours left
before we encounter
our uncomfortable ending.
So, let's fall asleep,
float face up,
and hold hands.
Beneath the chalky eye
of Hypnos,
we'll undulate
until tomorrow
finds us drifting apart.

Song of Washington Fog

She brings me spring
with her whisper
that sounds like the soft swoosh
of a pinwheel's spin.
It's then that her lower lip parts
from its perfect upper half,
and she brazenly bites mine.

Young pixie, you are a luxury,
and the staple of a passionate life.
Smart, svelte brunette,
keep me. Stretch over
my slender sides
and stay.

Stay,
for the day
does me no good
without your tender fingers
tapping me in time
to taper bad dreams.
Sugar,
absent your affection,
the dawn just ain't no sunrise.

Appalachian Andromeda

Andromeda,
your injuries are self-inflicted.
Perseus isn't flying
to your front door anymore.
Off-center, y'all are hate-entwined youth
who refuse to choose
a better lesson in letting go.

In this myth,
Perseus smokes too many cigarettes,
winged horse tattooed
across his broad shoulders.
He's harder.
The gent grows leaner
to leave her
without the same man
she met.

Today, he decides to get back to his bayou
instead of being tormented
by rumors of you.
The battle-worn soldier whistles
when wind
catches in the hollow places
where ventricles once were.

Where the Olympians
were epically clear:
When you feel your fancy going sideways,
cut her loose.

Andromeda,
those vindictive fingers
can't gash

a demi-god's carotid artery.
Perseus is in the clear,
but you
are terminally
trapped in fear.

Poem a Debutante Deserves

What you never knew
was that there was a classical prelude
that kept me in place
while we talked.
On a lone piano,
Liszt was with me
as I mellowed.

There wasn't a difficulty (at first).
The tedious moments leaked in later.
There was incessant chatter about social clubs,
faux-laughing tirades about the heart's idiocy,
and how many poems a debutante deserves.
(*Deserves?*)

I had a million ideas for our dialogue,
but your burdensome luxury
was a boomerang
that came back,
and *back*,
and back
instead of your favorite country song,
the weather,
or a comfortable silence.

My flow may seem madness,
but it is meticulous.
Your timeline for us
was in a hurry.
I reset the clock.
You laid down the law.
Without an ounce of hate,
I ducked out
and quickly cleaned the slate.

(*You deserve: 1*)

Prometheus, You are My Progeny

(for Dusty Huggins)

I.

The sky and brown thrasher
are inseparable.
Man calls this an illusion;
a feat of mathematics and perspective.

I see the placid mountain town
of Prometheus.
Do you?

II.

Definition is a point of contention.
Hours in knots over success
is banished into a brutal dark.
In August, that fact
allows
rivulets of light
to let doves take flight.
The only proof of their perch
is luminescent, terrestrial residue.

Gather fortitude
and fire, good son.
Become a righteousness
with little forgiveness.
I have too much guilt
to stay
in the left-hand lane,
and so do you.

Hang right, lock bad luck
in the glovebox,

and have a Coke.
There's always more room
for another
attempt at normalcy
and a tattoo.

III.

Squander no more days
on malaise.
Fasten your life vest
and realize
you can't reel in a woman
when she carries the darkest ocean
within her.

You are the shaman,
the postman;
in doubt due to a world
that does not work.
I have made it yield.
You will make it yield.

IV.

*The sky and brown thrasher
are inseparable.
Man calls this an illusion;
a feat of mathematics and perspective.*

*I call it
a wicked world of whimsy.
Do you?*

In the News

Hunched on a bench,
I read:
As violence falls in Iraq,
cemetery workers are earning less.
War is again men's
singular interest.

This mess only makes articles
that reference
revenge, our last stand,
and more details
about the Taliban.

I am weary of war.
War burdens the air.
Politically conscious songs
make me nauseated.
Writing poetry about it
is an art of breaking bricks.

I don't, but many argue
to stay angry.
They are squalling kids
that suddenly find life too scary.
America is anxious,
soul-sick.

Those cemetery workers
are jewels
in a land of ash.

The Original Title Failed Me

I may lie to my heart,
but my heart never lies to me.

—BEN HARPER AND CHARLIE MUSSELWHITE,
   "You've Found Another Lover (I've Lost Another Friend)"

I.

What's most uncommon
is your skin. The moment I brush it,
hold it close to my cheek,
the smooth calm of it
keeps me in stasis
when the world is usually
a blur. The entire of you has severe lines,
but not one hard edge.

This short drive to you
gives me the gap autos often provide
where I recollect how exotic you seemed
a week ago,
last night,
even
now
I think about
how your bangs frame
a profile Beatrice
would describe
as beautiful and brave.

You are foreign to me.
I didn't know then, little more now,
how to let what flows
deepest in me,
come loose to you. The wrenches for reaching

so far have been lost over the years.
Long in the tooth,
bitter feels frighteningly
permanent.

. . .

Young lady, I don't have a lexicon,
a pliable language
to let you know
you're like snow in June.

We shall always be suspicious things
to a species
stuck in neutral.
We are not them, sweet pea.
Give me one minute,
a cigarette, the excuse to steal a hug;
in those scant seconds
we are scarcely seen
in this busy cosmos.

Before dinner,
Jeff Buckley reminds us
to have faith. (*Hallelujah.*)
I realize the bedroom is our church.
A pearl necklace drapes
around your neck.
That perfume is brand new,
and it dents
my sense of decency.

II.

While rambling around Rome with you
I could sense
the college nearby I once enjoyed,
and the complicity between us.
Sunshine through a window
lights up the gold flecks
in your green eyes.

Traffic isn't creeping,
or tragic
in this hour slender in dissatisfaction,
and full of good feeling.
You, me—*it is different.*

III.

Untimely fireworks explode
in October, this evening,
due to a July
too wet to enjoy them.
We watch the wild display
and deem ourselves weird,
but we're
that perfect, complementary
kind of weird
where the heart
is wholly unhindered.

We are similar,
but not mathematically exact.
From that wellspring has

come our only poisonous discussions.
This is no complaint,
more a point of interest.
How do you interpret it?

You said:
I wish you'd allow yourself
time away from
the galaxy in your head,
and more time
in the stars with me.

The Collusion of Poet & Composer

When you witness
your guitar played
by someone else—
a slack-faced man who
gets those six strings to scream—
the quasi-honor is humbling.
It's an equally uneasy conflict
reminiscent of seeing
the one girl
you haven't gotten over
sitting in another guy's lap.

In the time it takes to listen,
no,
to *hear*
how lyrics come from pure sound,
there are miracles:
The mayor of Union Point makes coffee,
a bank teller starts his car,
two bluesmen
play one happy song.

Our band
has a psychologist
on piano,
an actor who loves-up a Les Paul,
and a recently freed felon
on sax.
Unaware of anyone else,
we consider when to end
our unrecorded opus.

In the last act
the tune is licked closed, adored,

and respectfully laid to rest.
That noise is knit into a pauper's pocket,
buried in the begging glory
of itself.

Overlooking Tom's Garden

As the seventh day descends,
African guineas
sneak up
from underbrush.
In Lexington.
all three look
mournful,
cluck, mill around
with their heads
down,
and cry
in low branches.

The abandoned siblings
seem anguished
over another
dying day
with their odd,
oval shapes misplaced;
killing time
while so far
from home.

Burning the Old Writer's Den

(for Holly Holt)

Tonight, I shed my ill-fit skin. Through threads that connect four walls, for three years, I only witnessed worry and anxious pacing. Soon this sepulcher shall be abandoned. My past is now a knot of a child's curtains kept only for kindling. There is no time for talk of potential, but rather action without the burden of offspring, poorly-trained pets, or relationships that lack the illumination of any embraceable light.

The seething silt that settles over my Garden of Letting Go allows me to grow gray within my wicked id—without apology. It sends a thicket of avarice across my chest, and massages out the mangled corners free from the creative malady. Hell, Purgatory, and Paradise are contained by the fine fit of a linen suit that I, the fiend, found dark enough to swallow greed. Any unhealed fissure that may remain (which fear forced open in my flesh) is fused closed by the virtue thistle in veins of this vicious man. *I am not without God.* It's just that all my soft, sensitive yesterdays are left on a dock where neglectful mothers leave children without a father to pick them up.

Phosphorus is struck against my rough thumb, and it allows this wreck-of-a-room to have its last dance, to burn, and no longer bind me to accept a man's business must be bad.

I spit, smoke, and then whip open the window. With irresponsible wings, this wraith rages into a night without nostalgia: not stinking of the secret I think settling is sadistic. I sink all my sickness-of-self in the lake my grandfather gave his kids, off the same shore where I grew up. Submerged beneath that familial, muddied water is the sorrow I nurtured for no reason.

My old writer's den is the last lethargic chain left by bad decisions. A shadow stays on its knees to pray and *pray* the sky sends angels. *Instead of whining, work harder*—leave no stone un-thrown. There's a pistol snug in the small of my back because too soon I will square off with the dead. I am certain of this. However, I am not then. I am now. I am this ride. I am this roll. My epidermis is armor I lacked before the War of Athena that reinforced the fact that society is useful, but not necessary. Blood is a wash of happenstance.

Knock-Off Authors Slink into Second Service

(for Jennifer Avery)

Me and my villains of verse
do not desire to drink and curse.
No, today a carnival soon comes
and artists gravitate toward Second Service.
Men and women worry
and try to pass off their
theatric poverty
by acting the musician,
the poet, the dancer who
can't find the right fans.

Those fools know
no fans fill seats for them.
Denial is their defense
against our dour disposition
for being hostages
to hear a generic
Greek tragedy.
I have no kin in this comedy,
so I sneak out to soak
up cigarette smoke.

Am I a lack of empathy? Yes.
What word best sums up those
who lost their Saturday
to lie to their sons concerning sonnets?
Stupid.

I look over Rome,
and see again it is a triangle
of rivers that rear up

an inspired wind.
It seeps up as a spell
that few tap into.
I sit and accept
this haunted hour.

The next sixty minutes
consist of sunlight,
stale air, and oppressed
by another bastard
who believes Bukowski is king.
I spot a plus-size seductress
I assume will vomit vampire poetry,
or how she hates penis.
(Mine hasn't hijacked or hung anyone.)

Why is it kosher to curse my
thin corpse,
but gluttony is forgiven
because a "gland" can't
cut out cake?
(I will be hated for this.)

I get more grief for having hair.
Called "gay" for being wifeless:
I didn't breed, so it *must* be.
No, it is because
I don't hate women.
I can't sire another soul of my cancer.
The truth of it
is too sharp a truth to divulge.
I do not want to read anymore.

I am not vain.
Vanity savors envy.
I find it vile.

So, to clear the chaos for kindness,
I stomp these negative thoughts
into the sidewalk
like a dead cigarette,
smile, and straighten my tie.

There are clowns
at every circus,
but we still attend
to see the acrobats.

French Flowers Unfurl in Georgia

(for Isabelle Gautier)

French flowers:
subtle in the center,
three pliable whirls
of purple
wink.

Unframed freshness, abstract flora,
hangs for an evening
in Georgia.
To personify the trio
as sassy ladies,
or preening men,
is a sin.
No,
it is itself: a painting.

In this gallery there is currency
not paid or pandered or sold,
but on the contrary:
Immortality takes center stage,
conjured by their creator's urgency
to be happy,
or be nothing.

The scene is serene, but not silent.
It exists in the easy company of an émigré,
living in Atlanta now.
She shares simplicity on canvas
the minimalist in me
must digest
alone.

Three violet starlets
stun the doldrums
dour down my brow.
She (the artist)
all of us—knowing or not—
need to see this Parisian freesia
frequently before closing.
It is itself: a painting.

French flowers:
subtle in the center,
three pliable whirls
of purple
wink.

Orpheus & Eurydice

Orpheus didn't deserve the desolate existence insisted upon him. The Divine of his time didn't abide too much happiness for anyone alive. Orpheus was a genius, but obstinate of the heart. He had no other love, and would let the world burn to keep Eurydice breathing. Eurydice perished. A satyr chased her into a tangle of asps. Her rock star lived alone. Orpheus rearranged his heart into a wicked machine. With only his lyre, the unlucky son-of-a-Muse ran madly into the abyss. Revenge is raised in the prettiest face.

To avenge Eurydice, a man planned this snatch-and-grab. Orpheus would hold all of hell hostage to have one dead too soon back home. The Underworld was run by a unwieldy deity not haunted by a healthy mentality: Hades had, and has, a gambler's stare, and hears a hanged-man's last prayers. They raped, stabbed, and seduced simply to stave off the death of life as a damned life. Orpheus knew the use of disinherited immortals: Every summer Orpheus played for perdition to take Death's mind off the months pomegranate seeds stole away Persephone.

Orpheus wasn't the first bad boy to catch the blues, but he'd be the first to shove his spite down a demigod's gullet. *Don't start none, won't be none.* Orpheus strolled into the inferno to make a wager, or wage a war. Cerberus would not serve as a deterrent this time. Not for this desolate gentleman. In fact, the hellhound with several unfed heads, stayed silent. The madman's musician stood still and insisted on slinging insults across the archway Hades arranged during its creation. The son of Olympia did not have any court to appeal his asp-assassination of Eurydice. *Eurydice was rightfully the property of the wholly perished.* The house always wins.

Hades had his leg thrown over the left arm of the throne. He enjoyed this. Persephone did not. Orpheus accused Hades of heresy. Hadn't Hell just had half a year of yearning over his half-hearted sweetheart? Orpheus: *I'm here to take my honey home.* Persephone put her hand on the devil's knee, and silently asked Eurydice set free.

Persephone put her faith in the hero, but Hades had no talent to give a shit about humans. Hades replied: *You play every day, Orpheus. You live for music, first. Your curse is that you can't have it all. However, I have respect for your predicament. I'll set you up with your young regret.* Hades held out a hand; and Eurydice emerged to embrace it. The musician almost lost his frosted cool. She barely remembered her Orpheus: her once-upon-a-time: her fool. So not-long ago it was, her living, wanting nothing, now fading, but not faded for good. Hades said aloud for lords and ladies: *She follows you, tough guy. Behind you, like Lot's secret leaving whose lover thought the Lord misleading. He was not. I am not. Such a mistake will kill you with grieving. Focus on my front door, and not on this vixen. Trust me, brother.* (Slap to the back.) *Up top, outside, not caught by Cerberus: She's forever free of me.* Of course Orpheus agreed. There's no confusion left by an illusion of choice.

Orpheus put one foot in front of the other. He never hesitated. He listened; he listened; *he listened.* The spectral linen Eurydice wore, silently swept the floor. Up stairs, unspeaking faces stared. The only sound was silence. Not a single *swoosh. Silence.* Then: The gates! The sun! Cerberus let them pass sans the fuss. The rascal was reckless in his rush for their second chance at fun. Eurydice had no reason to see this as anything but still a dying season. Orpheus leaped, spun, and finally fooled by footfalls...as she fell back three steps, four steps, five steps, six steps...

Eurydice smiled behind the veil that fit like tinfoil over cold rock. *Love, again, went straight to Hell.* Orpheus could not acknowledge his human folly. Hubris? Probably, but the state of Eurydice, her unhearing of him left no sorrow sparing, set loose a loss beyond what Orpheus called "acceptable cost". Languishing, he laid down with silence, and put his face to the tall grass.

Fading beneath phases of the moon, Orpheus pretends to hear her laugh.

The Transparent Mess of an Unbalanced Man

I do not know the temper or time
or tolerance—enough—
to swallow another shot of society.
My good sense lacks an inch of space
for stories written to argue
ignorance is the key to independence.

I am not an agent of havoc.
I am a harbinger
hardened against whistling arrows.
It is not personal.

The transparent mess I've
mopped up around my room
lacks the zygote and responsibility
of a self-reliant sociopath.
In time, the brothel I abandon
will be rebuilt as an altar,
and my legion left as archangels.
No hate, fantasy, or crucifixion:
My faith will pump no bad blood.

Creation is a hurricane of caring too much.
It's a mighty spool of sincerity
tightly wound without warm arms,
no laugh: It is a nervous tic. It is ambivalent.
Common man acts without consequences.
The cathedral of divine dissidence

keeps the beat with pain.
Enlightenment is excruciating,
and it insists you stay still,
or at least unnoticed.

The Savior does not
slight us for celebrating
the pleasures
He openly provides. (Moderation)
My epigenetics catch that, chew,
and conclude that stereotypes are unfortunate,
but often earned.
Act the opposite and be the exception.

I swing the proper tackle
to stand above any oppressor.
The present, as the past,
is, and will be, absurd.

My skin is the color of a slave owner,
and my slim shape said to be sinister.
I have all the earmarks
allowed to be hated.
However,
I am not the whip or one owned.
I do not accept that
ancient obligation.
I feel it is an ordeal worth arguing
never.

I long-severed my empathy
for their self-induced conflict.
I am not in their
uncouth cult.
I am the cold shovel

cherished by an undertaker.
I am not injured
by the envy
of idiots.

Two Spirits Shake Off the Sun

a myth made of moonlight

Mundus vult decipi, ergo decipiatur.

Sunset:
There is a delicate current
that tonight
bites with new torment.
Her:
A lady is unsteady. Her ship adrift
on an ocean
she deems an accident
her will didn't put in motion.
Him:
The man is a simple myth-maker.

A woman:
Her hair is made of midnight,
but in her braids
are bluebells picked in Spain.
Growing free, Japanese anemone
still smell of sunshine,
and its petals kiss his bliss
into her amber eyes.
Sorrow cannot lay claim to her cerulean skies.

A man:
He is all the land
that spans from her heartbeat
to a heron's shape that seeps
silently into mist.

On the shore
is a cabin kept in a stand of shadows.
It is hallow ground
that allows only one sound—Silence.
His hands planted the
aster, goldenrod, and monkshood
that the wind whispers in scent
over her eyelids. now blows in plumes
over her pillows.

She is the whole of his wonder—
waltzing, wanting
to witness a sleep deeper than their despair.
On tip-toe she eases along
a towline he hammered into the moon
to prevent the morning
from dawning too soon.

Nightingales will not allow
the lark to sing,
and so romance will be their only season.
The day is banished.
The girl is lavished with secrets.
Oh,
to be beyond common men,
to see simple women sin somewhere else,
to exist without a need to believe in fate.
(That is the truth of it.
It is the conquest of their unconquerable spirit.)

A Symphony for Tracy Lee

A hotel room rocked
before it hummed to sleep.
The door stuck.
View from the 21st floor: All of Atlanta.
Dinner was done up
barely by daybreak.
Morning, little sleep: Cerebral snippets.
Tracy Lee,
These memories keep me thinking
new, almost-smudgeless,
stained-glass things.

Enamored by freedom,
we feel unafraid of the responsibility.
The weight of being right
sits beside us,
not in us.

I am, like the first words passion inflicted:
You're unrestricted.
We've screamed and slung sponges
in a spat.

So, I howl in a not-so-wicked way.
I wrench a moment back with that drunk,
but its function is purely pragmatic.
There is no cold in us. There is none
of the frost loathing leaves
until there's no lividity.
No. No. No. I howl as we are the
unrumpled grass, still air, and you.
We breathe.
This evening is simple.

Tonight, and for all nights,
you are a clean moonlight firefly,
throwing stars across the yard.

My pulmonary pear and its experience,
its palpitations, the interrogations before
we met in an autumn garden,
flush with no color—would confess. Anything, confess.
For me it's a rolling meadow of yellow maples.
Hyacinths grew in winter.
Lamb's ear is bunched around a tree stump.

In the river I revered
our reflection. Ours:
I am not as narcissistic
as some might think;
one acquaintance called it outright.
There's nothing wrong with that.

I am in the woods
as light breaking
through trees.
I am a fish
in a falcon's bill.
You are the wise whippoorwill.

My name? I have no name.
I have no lame foot to blame.
To live aloof is the key.
This distance isn't a curse,
it's my unquenchable need.
Either as a good son or bad seed,
I should feel, work, and stand
alone before reaching for a fairer hand.

All amore aside, this is a story:
It tells of a dark-haired lady
tough as smoothed, pine knots.
She is an orchid.
She reads like my favorite books.

Spring is not a season;
it is a sense of self.
More flesh appeals
in the warmth
than apples do in Georgia.
I chase your peaches.
I do.

We will come again,
here;
three dozen times,
come here.
We'll make love
in a hammock,
owe no one,
and know why Otis Redding
pleaded for tenderness
because *you just gotta try a little* . . .
Our estate will encase us,
as will tenderness,
and we will enjoy
anonymity.

We will come here again,
here;
three thousand more times,

come here.
There's no love without it.
There's no love
without
you.

Mid-Breaks for Rooster

Desperately, he dashes away from Alabama,
and the best, bad man's
guess is that it's 6 am; yet,
there are twenty more miles 'til Montgomery.
Miss New Orleans ought to be in Augusta,
Rooster reasons.
Yet it's widely known
that Georgia's neglectful nights
never recollect a man's righteousness.
The lies live forever.

Rooster's lack of virtue
stays shrouded beneath vultures.
His shoulders
both show bullet wounds.

The whole damned debacle
is due to dirty cops and a congressman.
You see, to live in a land
like Louisiana,
people are objects, money is heavy,
and illegitimate children
are pinned on a crook
named Rooster.

. . .

Rooster:
He plans to marry
Ms. New Orleans.
Inside a shotgun home
she works and writes his real name.
He is a kind crook
who creates their landscape

out of larceny.
The death he's dealt
is hearsay.

Rooster escapes police raids,
but always
wakes up worn out.
The sun washes off sin,
while coffee and humidity
blend into second-wind Zen.
He wants to put away his suitcase.
The rascal aches to hang his rifle.
Rooster struggles to shake
the shroud of a scoundrel too proud.
She pouts, stays out,
and keeps a knapsack in the car.

Ms. New Orleans was last heard
to make a home in Atlanta.
However,
the sullen anti-hero stays in Savannah.
By the church or other side tracks
not all who travel make it back.
It looks like
the cost of love
is leaving.

I Am Doc Holliday

(for T. C. Carter)

At 38 I realize my only lasting remedy
is to find a new, steady trail to follow.
A dozen haughty poseurs watch me,
peeking from behind the tallest pine.
I toast all those bastards
with a bottle of Spanish red wine,
cast a final glance behind,
then sing Sinatra
to woo the devil into more time.

Tonight this wrung-out-sad-man
drops his sack, straps on the boots
and lean shadow of a cowboy
that carries two Colts for the sinister spirits
in his memory's employ.
It's time to toss off Athens concrete
for freedom's scent,
and a patch of grass where no one
bitches over the government.

Gone,
sisters and brothers—gone:
A few books in a satchel off my horse's side,
I ride without an excuse to my name.
Don't eat much with all the brambles inside.
I am best alone so's not to leave
such a broken line behind.
The way she feels has never
weighed much on my mind.

That is my incurable infection.

I'll write Momma on her birthday.
Daddy will understand.
Myth creates an imperfectly-perfect land.
Both of 'em know my bones are rough
from ruthless thrill.
There's no getting right with God
while sitting still.

I'm not running from the past,
or mourning she who loved me last.
This is a journey away from a life
where I refused to raise a child,
and instead shoveled coal.
You do just about anything to pay rent,
and buckle down your soul.

Whether this is Frost's divided path
or Dante's dark wood,
I will wander them all as a true rambler should.
Few will notice I've chosen to see
all the open pastures alongside T.C.
Simple, eternal, forgotten, unseen,
near a river, quiet wind, both hands washed clean.

In the South

Cicadas
offer no history, only
a permanent revolution of seasons—
a melody,
a natural catastrophe.

. . .

Our loose thoughts combined after I told you
about the blond vagabond playing Vivaldi downtown
with only his toes touching the ground,
how the soothing sounds those strings
spread were his roots among us
that challenged reality; in it
he was the only soul entangled.

His violin was spotless, though he was not—
he was a stalagmite, vapor, the remnants of awful parents,
vacant eyes, gaping mouth.

Unkempt, he was another time-wasted thing, disintegrating
from an inability to remain tangible, shadows crowding 'round,
same as you see on the road home through Yazoo, Waco, and
Monroe, impassable because your headlights always shined
behind . . . *nevertheless*—a surreal sight on Hancock, that man

like the dark wood of a dining table, primer still smelling
of orange blossoms wiped up in dusty plumes, letters propped up
against a vase beneath the bowing heads of crested irises,
nearby is grandfather's photo in black and white,
expensive parchment for better letters is unused.

Today, for me, a lady is a fading reflection as I look out
from a sturdy frame; the air is filled with cynicism.
For years I collected specters in a blue Bible,
and tonight I give them all to Vivaldi's madman.
Those motels, the lying sleep, this time to mend:
They are forgotten secrets between us and lunacy.
They are no longer yours.
They are no longer mine.

. . .

Cicadas
play to help remember, keeping
time the way a metronome does:
Not to pass the hour,
but hone its rhythm.
They are blades that slice away
what I don't want.

Clifford Brooks was born in Athens, Georgia. His first poetry collection, *The Draw of Broken Eyes & Whirling Metaphysics,* nominated for a Georgia Author of the Year Award in Poetry, will be re-issued by Kudzu Leaf Press in 2018. His limited-edition poetry chapbook *Exiles of Eden* was published in 2017, also by Kudzu Leaf Press. Clifford is the founder of The Southern Collective Experience, a cooperative of writers, musicians and visual artists, which publishes the journal *The Blue Mountain Review* and hosts the radio show *Dante's Old South.* He currently lives in northwest Georgia and is pursuing an MFA in Creative Writing at Reinhardt University.

www.cliffbrooks.com